■SCHOLASTIC

W9-CLF-206

FAST FACTS MULTIPLICATION & DIVISION

by Susan Dillon

New York • Toronto • London • Auckland • Sydney
Mexico City • New Delhi • Hong Kong • Buenos Aires

Teaching Resources

To my Math for Laughs students and teachers—
you are always inspiring!

Cover design by Jannie Ho

Interior design by Ellen Matlach for Boultinghouse & Boultinghouse, Inc.

Interior illustrations by Teresa Anderko

ISBN-13 978-0-439-54886-1
ISBN-10 0-439-54886-1

6 7 8 9 10   40   14 13 12 11 10

Contents

Introduction

It's a fact: Students need to know their math facts! According to the Principles and Standards for School Mathematics published by the National Council on the Teaching of Mathematics (NCTM), fluency is a critical goal: "By *fluency* we mean that students are able to compute efficiently and accurately with single-digit numbers." One way to achieve this fluency is to practice.

Inspired by my fifth-grade son and my work with elementary-age children, I created *Fast Facts* based on the idea that students love a race. Whether it's a friendly game with classmates or measuring their own self-improvement, students get pumped up for practice when you throw in a little healthy competition as incentive.

This book contains reproducible activity sheets to reinforce your lessons and get students on track to faster mental computation of addition and subtraction facts. Each section includes four sheets. The first one is easiest (rated level 1), the second is more difficult (level 2), and the third contains the most difficult problems (level 3). The last features blanks that you can fill in with any problems you choose. All activity sheets contain 18 problems.

Knowing math facts is a key building block to advanced math, and to a lifetime of mental math competency. NCTM states: "Ambitious standards are required to achieve a society that has the capability to think and reason mathematically. . . ." From tallying a grocery bill to estimating the mileage of the drive to the store—without a calculator—students will use these skills for the rest of their lives.

So . . . have fun with the fast facts!

Racetrack

How can students see and celebrate improvement? There are several ways students can track their speed and accuracy as you use certain favorite activity sheets from this book again and again.

To improve students' facts calculations, assign the same activity sheet every day for three days or more as classwork or homework. Make plenty of photocopies! Let students keep track of their own improvement with the Racetrack on page 7.

Speed

Before beginning the activity sheet, students should go to the stopwatch icon, located at the bottom left corner of the activity sheet. Direct students to fill in the number of minutes and seconds they will have to solve the problems. You can take care of the timing. Students will complete as many problems accurately as possible. There are different ways you can approach this. For example, if you start the activity with 10 minutes to complete the sheet, each time you revisit the same activity, you can reduce the amount of allotted time gradually. Or, if you start the activity with 1 minute, each time you revisit the activity, students can try to increase the number of problems they can solve in that time.

Accuracy

Emphasize that while the goal is for work to be done quickly it must also be done accurately. Each activity sheet has a bull's eye at the bottom right corner. This area is for recording the accuracy of the work done (the total answers minus the incorrect answers equals the correct answers). You can fill in this section, or students can grade their own sheets while you call out the correct answers from the answer key (page 48). Depending on the needs of your students, you can also create and display an answer key for individual activity sheets by filling in the answers and copying the completed sheet onto an overhead transparency.

Assessment

Even the youngest students can maintain their own Racetrack (page 7) with some guidance. They can judge for themselves if they were faster and/or more accurate than the last race. Ask them to compare their speed and accuracy for this race with the last race: "Did you get more answers right this time?" Or, pointing to the time, ask: "Do you think this number is smaller than this number? If so, that means you were faster!" Feel free to urge students who experience a one-time nose-dive in speed or accuracy to try a race again. After completing the required races, ask students: "How did you do?" Let them answer in their own words.

Challenge

Note that activity sheets in each section gradually increase in difficulty depending on grade-appropriate content. You may want to skip to more challenging sheets for older students. Keep in mind though that the easiest sheets are great speed practice for even the most advanced students. Since the activity sheets have 18 problems, consider cutting some problems for the youngest students. When revisiting an activity sheet multiple times, you can make it different and more challenging by asking students to complete answers right to left, bottom to top, or starting somewhere in the middle of the activity (for instance, "start at the letter *d*"). Use the blank sheet to write problems that are better geared toward your lessons.

Motivation

Photocopy and distribute at least one copy per student of the racetrack on page 7. Students should write their name in the space provided on the racetrack, along with the name of the activity sheet they will use. Students also get a new copy of a racer icon each time they complete an activity sheet. On the icon, they should write Race 1, Race 2, Race 3, and so on. Choose from the reproducible samples on page 6 or have students draw their own. A racer begins on the starting line (attach to individual tracks with tape).

The track is divided into 18 segments,

matching the number of problems on the activity sheet. Students can indicate their progress by attaching a racer to the segment that represents the number of problems they solved accurately within an allotted time. The goal is to increase this number, getting closer to the finish line (18 correct answers).

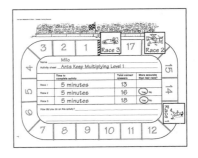

The number of segments you include can also relate to the number of times you plan to use a certain sheet. For example, if you direct students to complete the "Ants Keep Multiplying Level 1" sheet three times in three days, the track could be divided into thirds. In this case, students only use one copy of a racer icon. If a student improves timing and/or accuracy, she or he should take the racer and put it in the next segment on the track, advancing toward the finish.

Either way you approach the activities, encourage students' improvement with medals! You can buy these at any party goods store. Or, use the reproducible version on page 6 and attach directly to students' shirts with tape, or with a safety pin attached to the back of the cut-out with masking tape. Using a rubber stamp with a simple, positive saying such as "Great effort!" or "Wow!" is also an effective way to motivate students or acknowledge their improvement.

6

Name _____

Activity sheet _____

	Time to complete activity	Total correct answers	More accurate than last race?
Race 1			
Race 2			Yes No
Race 3			Yes No

How did you do on this activity? _____
_____

Multiplex Solutions

LEVEL 1

At the new multiplex movie theater in town, you need to multiply correctly in order to get your tickets. Solve the problems and enjoy the show. *Try to get those facts fast!*

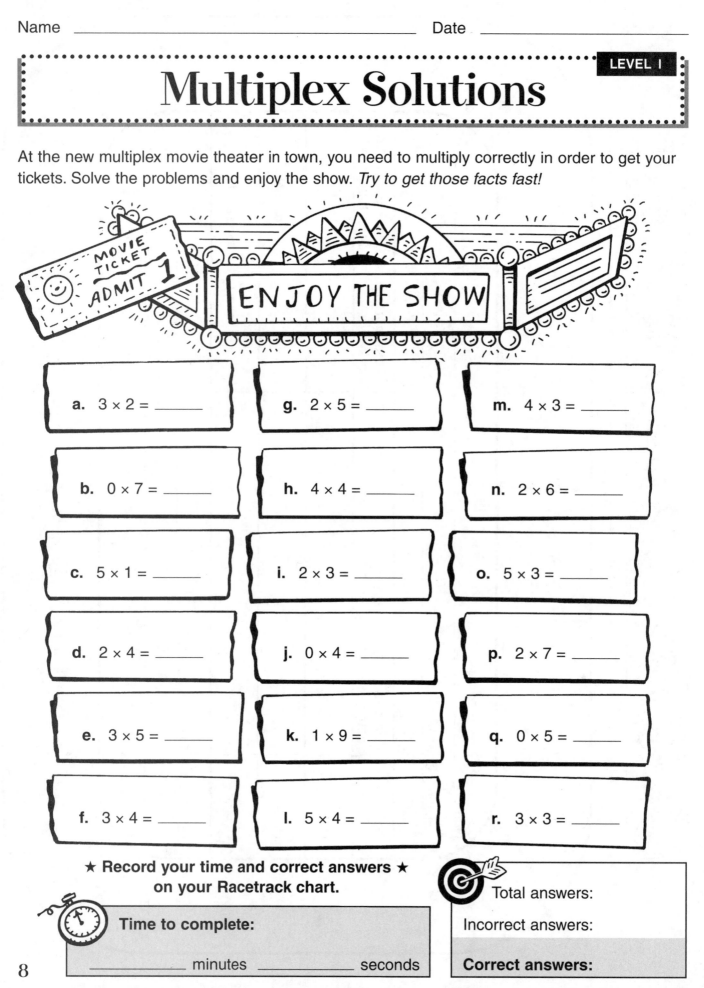

MOVIE TICKET
ADMIT 1

ENJOY THE SHOW

a. $3 \times 2 =$ _____

b. $0 \times 7 =$ _____

c. $5 \times 1 =$ _____

d. $2 \times 4 =$ _____

e. $3 \times 5 =$ _____

f. $3 \times 4 =$ _____

g. $2 \times 5 =$ _____

h. $4 \times 4 =$ _____

i. $2 \times 3 =$ _____

j. $0 \times 4 =$ _____

k. $1 \times 9 =$ _____

l. $5 \times 4 =$ _____

m. $4 \times 3 =$ _____

n. $2 \times 6 =$ _____

o. $5 \times 3 =$ _____

p. $2 \times 7 =$ _____

q. $0 \times 5 =$ _____

r. $3 \times 3 =$ _____

★ **Record your time and correct answers** ★
on your Racetrack chart.

Time to complete:

_____ minutes _____ seconds

Total answers:

Incorrect answers:

Correct answers:

8

Fast Facts: Multiplication & Division Scholastic Teaching Resources

Name _____ Date _____

Multiplex Solutions

At the new multiplex movie theater in town, you need to multiply correctly in order to get your tickets. Solve the problems and enjoy the show. *Try to get those facts fast!*

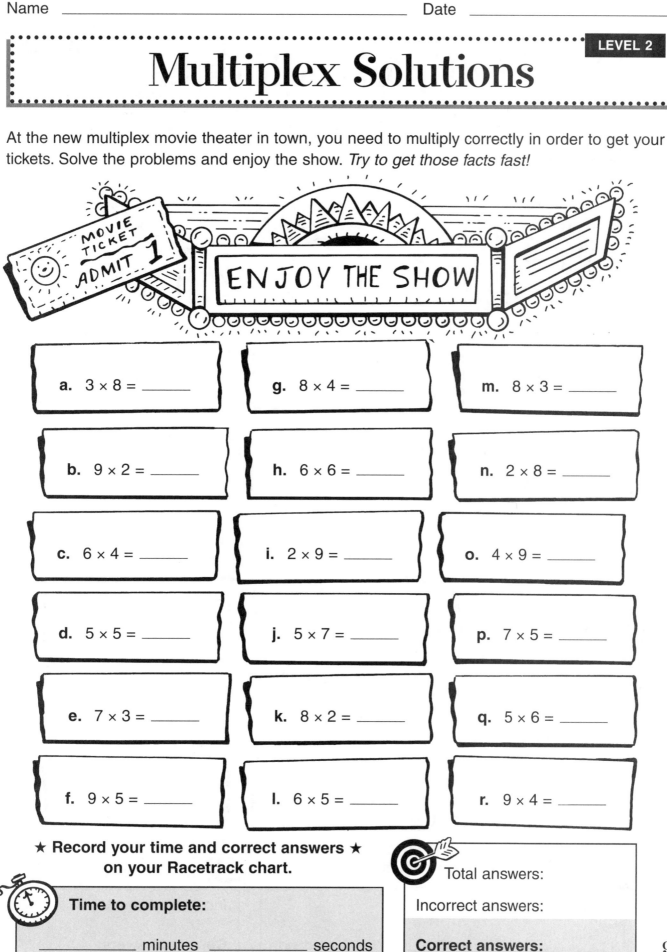

ENJOY THE SHOW

a. $3 \times 8 =$ _____

b. $9 \times 2 =$ _____

c. $6 \times 4 =$ _____

d. $5 \times 5 =$ _____

e. $7 \times 3 =$ _____

f. $9 \times 5 =$ _____

g. $8 \times 4 =$ _____

h. $6 \times 6 =$ _____

i. $2 \times 9 =$ _____

j. $5 \times 7 =$ _____

k. $8 \times 2 =$ _____

l. $6 \times 5 =$ _____

m. $8 \times 3 =$ _____

n. $2 \times 8 =$ _____

o. $4 \times 9 =$ _____

p. $7 \times 5 =$ _____

q. $5 \times 6 =$ _____

r. $9 \times 4 =$ _____

★ **Record your time and correct answers** ★
on your Racetrack chart.

Time to complete:

_____ minutes _____ seconds

Total answers:

Incorrect answers:

Correct answers:

Name _____ Date _____

Multiplex Solutions

At the new multiplex movie theater in town, you need to multiply correctly in order to get your tickets. Solve the problems and enjoy the show. *Try to get those facts fast!*

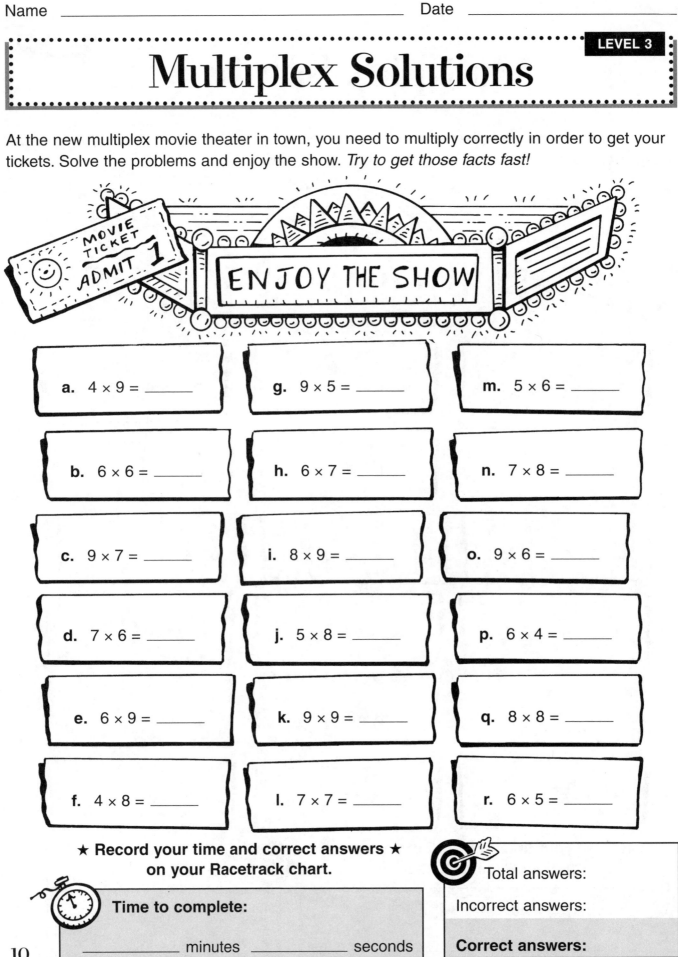

a. 4 × 9 = _____

b. 6 × 6 = _____

c. 9 × 7 = _____

d. 7 × 6 = _____

e. 6 × 9 = _____

f. 4 × 8 = _____

g. 9 × 5 = _____

h. 6 × 7 = _____

i. 8 × 9 = _____

j. 5 × 8 = _____

k. 9 × 9 = _____

l. 7 × 7 = _____

m. 5 × 6 = _____

n. 7 × 8 = _____

o. 9 × 6 = _____

p. 6 × 4 = _____

q. 8 × 8 = _____

r. 6 × 5 = _____

★ **Record your time and correct answers** ★
on your Racetrack chart.

Time to complete:

_____ minutes _____ seconds

Total answers:

Incorrect answers:

Correct answers:

10

Fast Facts: Multiplication & Division Scholastic Teaching Resources

Name _____   Date _____

Multiplex Solutions

At the new multiplex movie theater in town, you need to multiply correctly in order to get your tickets. Solve the problems and enjoy the show. *Try to get those facts fast!*

a. ___ × ___ = _____

b. ___ × ___ = _____

c. ___ × ___ = _____

d. ___ × ___ = _____

e. ___ × ___ = _____

f. ___ × ___ = _____

g. ___ × ___ = _____

h. ___ × ___ = _____

i. ___ × ___ = _____

j. ___ × ___ = _____

k. ___ × ___ = _____

l. ___ × ___ = _____

m. ___ × ___ = _____

n. ___ × ___ = _____

o. ___ × ___ = _____

p. ___ × ___ = _____

q. ___ × ___ = _____

r. ___ × ___ = _____

★ **Record your time and correct answers** ★
on your Racetrack chart.

Time to complete:

_____ minutes _____ seconds

Total answers: _____

Incorrect answers: _____

Correct answers: _____

Fast Facts: Multiplication & Division   Scholastic Teaching Resources

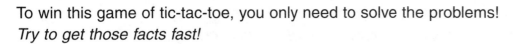

LEVEL I

Multi-Tac-Toe

To win this game of tic-tac-toe, you only need to solve the problems!
Try to get those facts fast!

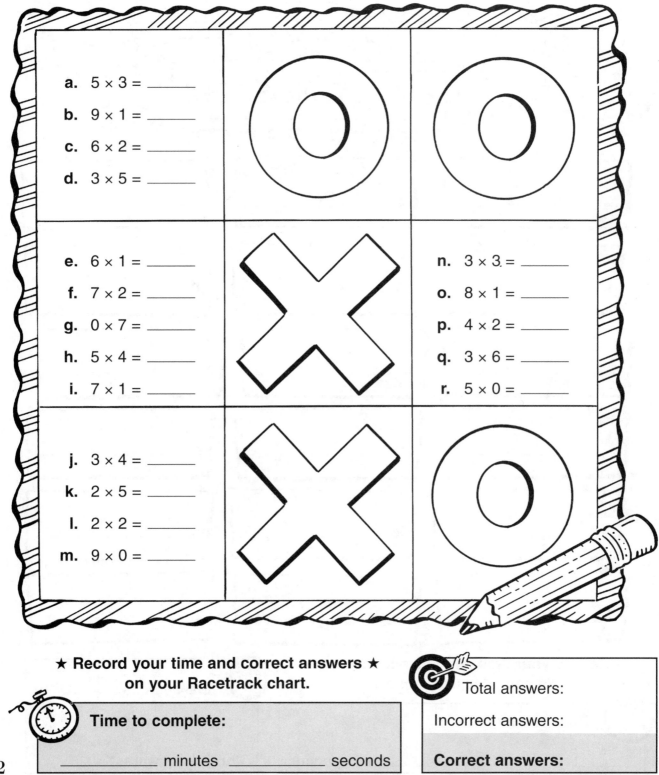

a. 5 × 3 = _____

b. 9 × 1 = _____

c. 6 × 2 = _____

d. 3 × 5 = _____

e. 6 × 1 = _____

f. 7 × 2 = _____

g. 0 × 7 = _____

h. 5 × 4 = _____

i. 7 × 1 = _____

n. 3 × 3 = _____

o. 8 × 1 = _____

p. 4 × 2 = _____

q. 3 × 6 = _____

r. 5 × 0 = _____

j. 3 × 4 = _____

k. 2 × 5 = _____

l. 2 × 2 = _____

m. 9 × 0 = _____

★ **Record your time and correct answers** ★
on your Racetrack chart.

Time to complete:

_____ minutes _____ seconds

Total answers:

Incorrect answers:

Correct answers:

Fast Facts: Multiplication & Division Scholastic Teaching Resources

Name _____ Date _____

Multi-Tac-Toe

To win this game of tic-tac-toe, you only need to solve the problems!
Try to get those facts fast!

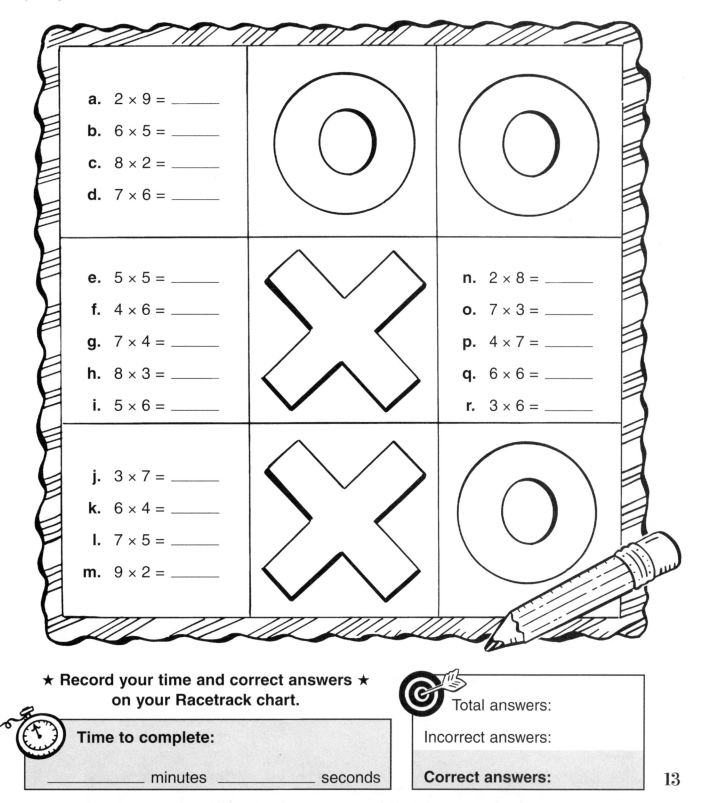

a. 2 × 9 = _____

b. 6 × 5 = _____

c. 8 × 2 = _____

d. 7 × 6 = _____

e. 5 × 5 = _____

f. 4 × 6 = _____

g. 7 × 4 = _____

h. 8 × 3 = _____

i. 5 × 6 = _____

n. 2 × 8 = _____

o. 7 × 3 = _____

p. 4 × 7 = _____

q. 6 × 6 = _____

r. 3 × 6 = _____

j. 3 × 7 = _____

k. 6 × 4 = _____

l. 7 × 5 = _____

m. 9 × 2 = _____

★ **Record your time and correct answers** ★
on your Racetrack chart.

Time to complete:

_____ minutes _____ seconds

Total answers:

Incorrect answers:

Correct answers:

Name _____   Date _____

Multi-Tac-Toe

To win this game of tic-tac-toe, you only need to solve the problems!
Try to get those facts fast!

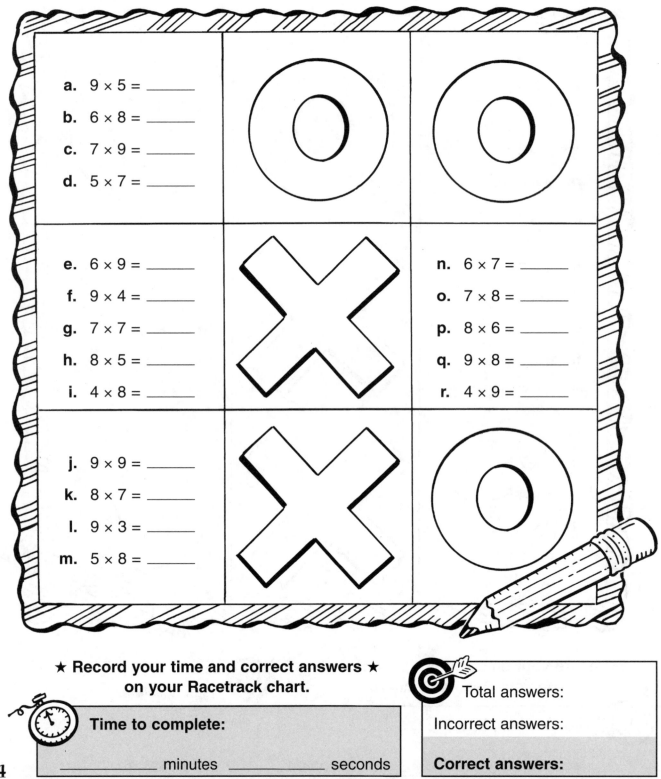

a. $9 \times 5 =$ _____	
b. $6 \times 8 =$ _____	
c. $7 \times 9 =$ _____	
d. $5 \times 7 =$ _____	

e. $6 \times 9 =$ _____	**n.** $6 \times 7 =$ _____
f. $9 \times 4 =$ _____	**o.** $7 \times 8 =$ _____
g. $7 \times 7 =$ _____	**p.** $8 \times 6 =$ _____
h. $8 \times 5 =$ _____	**q.** $9 \times 8 =$ _____
i. $4 \times 8 =$ _____	**r.** $4 \times 9 =$ _____

j. $9 \times 9 =$ _____
k. $8 \times 7 =$ _____
l. $9 \times 3 =$ _____
m. $5 \times 8 =$ _____

★ **Record your time and correct answers** ★
on your Racetrack chart.

Time to complete:

_____ minutes _____ seconds

Total answers:

Incorrect answers:

Correct answers:

Fast Facts: Multiplication & Division   Scholastic Teaching Resources

Name _____ Date _____

Multi-Tac-Toe

To win this game of tic-tac-toe, you only need to solve the problems!
Try to get those facts fast!

a. ___ × ___ = ___

b. ___ × ___ = ___

c. ___ × ___ = ___

d. ___ × ___ = ___

e. ___ × ___ = ___

f. ___ × ___ = ___

g. ___ × ___ = ___

h. ___ × ___ = ___

i. ___ × ___ = ___

n. ___ × ___ = ___

o. ___ × ___ = ___

p. ___ × ___ = ___

q. ___ × ___ = ___

r. ___ × ___ = ___

j. ___ × ___ = ___

k. ___ × ___ = ___

l. ___ × ___ = ___

m. ___ × ___ = ___

★ **Record your time and correct answers ★
   on your Racetrack chart.**

Time to complete:

_____ minutes _____ seconds

Total answers:

Incorrect answers:

Correct answers:

Name _____   Date _____

Ants Keep Multiplying

There are ants everywhere, and they've come to eat your picnic lunch. Solve as many problems as you can before they take the goodies away. *Try to get those facts fast!*

a. $3 \times 1 =$ _____

b. $5 \times 2 =$ _____

f. $0 \times 9 =$ _____

g. $3 \times 5 =$ _____

h. $2 \times 4 =$ _____

i. $1 \times 6 =$ _____

c. $4 \times 0 =$ _____

d. $3 \times 4 =$ _____

e. $1 \times 7 =$ _____

j. $5 \times 0 =$ _____

k. $2 \times 6 =$ _____

l. $1 \times 3 =$ _____

m. $4 \times 3 =$ _____

n. $2 \times 2 =$ _____

o. $5 \times 4 =$ _____

p. $0 \times 8 =$ _____

q. $3 \times 7 =$ _____

r. $3 \times 3 =$ _____

★ **Record your time and correct answers** ★
on your Racetrack chart.

Time to complete:

_____ minutes _____ seconds

Total answers:

Incorrect answers:

Correct answers:

Fast Facts: Multiplication & Division Scholastic Teaching Resources

Name _____ Date _____

There are ants everywhere, and they've come to eat your picnic lunch. Solve as many problems as you can before they take the goodies away. *Try to get those facts fast!*

a. $4 \times 6 =$ _____

b. $7 \times 2 =$ _____

c. $9 \times 3 =$ _____

d. $3 \times 8 =$ _____

e. $5 \times 6 =$ _____

f. $7 \times 4 =$ _____

g. $8 \times 2 =$ _____

h. $5 \times 7 =$ _____

i. $4 \times 9 =$ _____

j. $6 \times 3 =$ _____

k. $8 \times 4 =$ _____

l. $9 \times 5 =$ _____

m. $2 \times 9 =$ _____

n. $4 \times 8 =$ _____

o. $7 \times 3 =$ _____

p. $8 \times 5 =$ _____

q. $3 \times 7 =$ _____

r. $6 \times 6 =$ _____

★ **Record your time and correct answers** ★
on your Racetrack chart.

Time to complete:

_____ minutes _____ seconds

Total answers: _____

Incorrect answers: _____

Correct answers: _____

Fast Facts: Multiplication & Division Scholastic Teaching Resources

Name _____ Date _____

Ants Keep Multiplying

There are ants everywhere, and they've come to eat your picnic lunch. Solve as many problems as you can before they take the goodies away. *Try to get those facts fast!*

a. $6 \times 9 =$ _____

b. $9 \times 5 =$ _____

c. $6 \times 6 =$ _____

d. $8 \times 4 =$ _____

e. $4 \times 9 =$ _____

f. $3 \times 9 =$ _____

g. $8 \times 7 =$ _____

h. $9 \times 9 =$ _____

i. $4 \times 8 =$ _____

j. $6 \times 5 =$ _____

k. $8 \times 8 =$ _____

l. $6 \times 8 =$ _____

m. $9 \times 7 =$ _____

n. $4 \times 7 =$ _____

o. $8 \times 9 =$ _____

p. $6 \times 7 =$ _____

q. $8 \times 5 =$ _____

r. $7 \times 8 =$ _____

★ **Record your time and correct answers** ★
on your Racetrack chart.

Time to complete:

_____ minutes _____ seconds

Total answers: _____

Incorrect answers: _____

Correct answers: _____

18

Fast Facts: Multiplication & Division   Scholastic Teaching Resources

Name _____   Date _____

Ants Keep Multiplying

There are ants everywhere, and they've come to eat your picnic lunch. Solve as many problems as you can before they take the goodies away. *Try to get those facts fast!*

a. ___ × ___ = ___

b. ___ × ___ = ___

f. ___ × ___ = ___

g. ___ × ___ = ___

h. ___ × ___ = ___

i. ___ × ___ = ___

c. ___ × ___ = ___

d. ___ × ___ = ___

e. ___ × ___ = ___

j. ___ × ___ = ___

k. ___ × ___ = ___

l. ___ × ___ = ___

m. ___ × ___ = ___

n. ___ × ___ = ___

o. ___ × ___ = ___

p. ___ × ___ = ___

q. ___ × ___ = ___

r. ___ × ___ = ___

★ **Record your time and correct answers** ★
on your Racetrack chart.

Time to complete:

_____ minutes _____ seconds

Total answers: _____

Incorrect answers: _____

Correct answers: _____

Fast Facts: Multiplication & Division Scholastic Teaching Resources

Name _____ Date _____

Time for Times!

What time is it? Time to time doing times! Solve the problems. *Try to get those facts fast!*

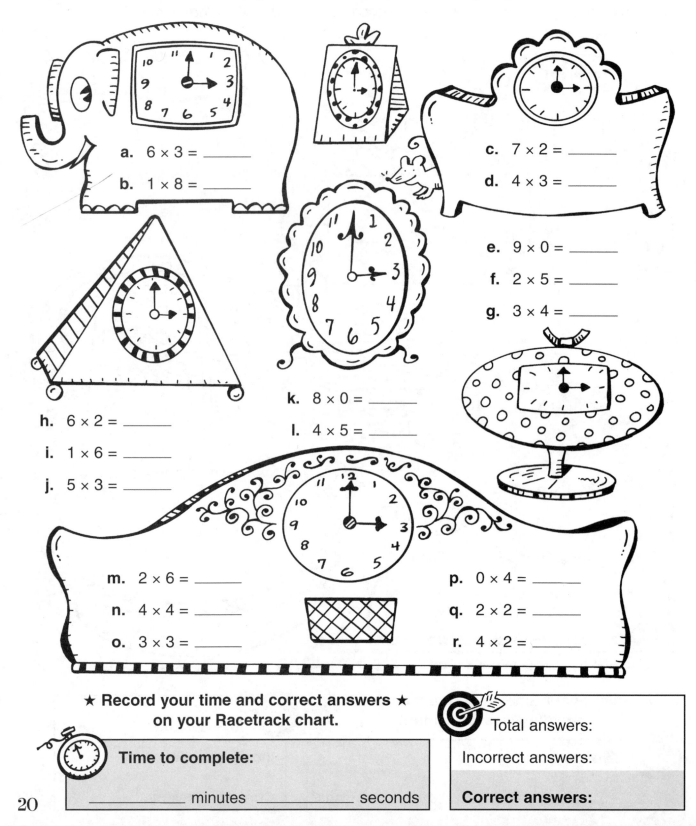

a. $6 \times 3 =$ _____

b. $1 \times 8 =$ _____

c. $7 \times 2 =$ _____

d. $4 \times 3 =$ _____

e. $9 \times 0 =$ _____

f. $2 \times 5 =$ _____

g. $3 \times 4 =$ _____

h. $6 \times 2 =$ _____

i. $1 \times 6 =$ _____

j. $5 \times 3 =$ _____

k. $8 \times 0 =$ _____

l. $4 \times 5 =$ _____

m. $2 \times 6 =$ _____

n. $4 \times 4 =$ _____

o. $3 \times 3 =$ _____

p. $0 \times 4 =$ _____

q. $2 \times 2 =$ _____

r. $4 \times 2 =$ _____

★ **Record your time and correct answers** ★
on your Racetrack chart.

Time to complete:

_____ minutes _____ seconds

Total answers: _____

Incorrect answers: _____

Correct answers:

20

Fast Facts: Multiplication & Division Scholastic Teaching Resources

Name _____ Date _____

Time for Times!

What time is it? Time to time doing times! Solve the problems. *Try to get those facts fast!*

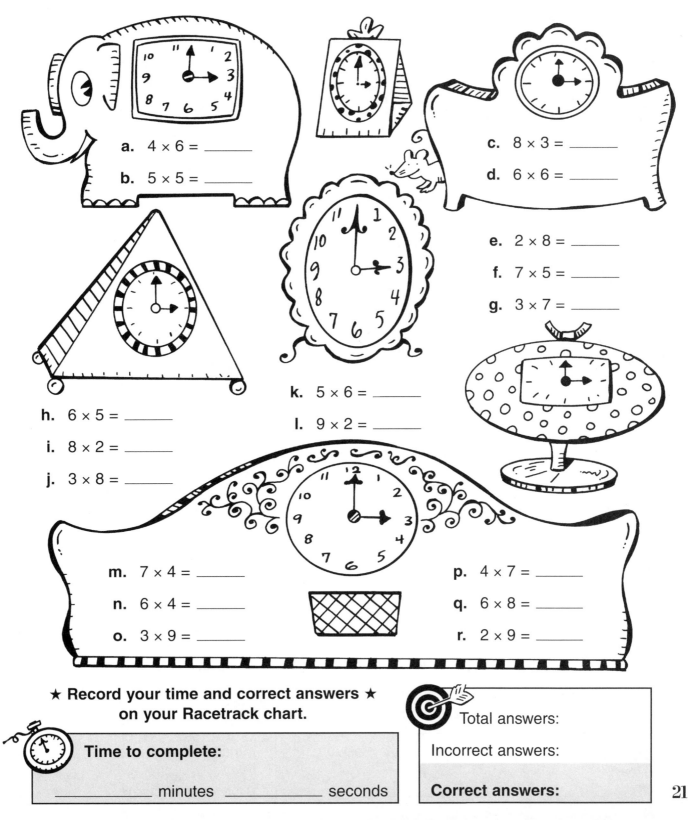

a. 4 × 6 = _____

b. 5 × 5 = _____

c. 8 × 3 = _____

d. 6 × 6 = _____

e. 2 × 8 = _____

f. 7 × 5 = _____

g. 3 × 7 = _____

h. 6 × 5 = _____

i. 8 × 2 = _____

j. 3 × 8 = _____

k. 5 × 6 = _____

l. 9 × 2 = _____

m. 7 × 4 = _____

n. 6 × 4 = _____

o. 3 × 9 = _____

p. 4 × 7 = _____

q. 6 × 8 = _____

r. 2 × 9 = _____

★ **Record your time and correct answers** ★
on your Racetrack chart.

Time to complete:

_____ minutes _____ seconds

Total answers:

Incorrect answers:

Correct answers:

Time for Times!

What time is it? Time to time doing times! Solve the problems. *Try to get those facts fast!*

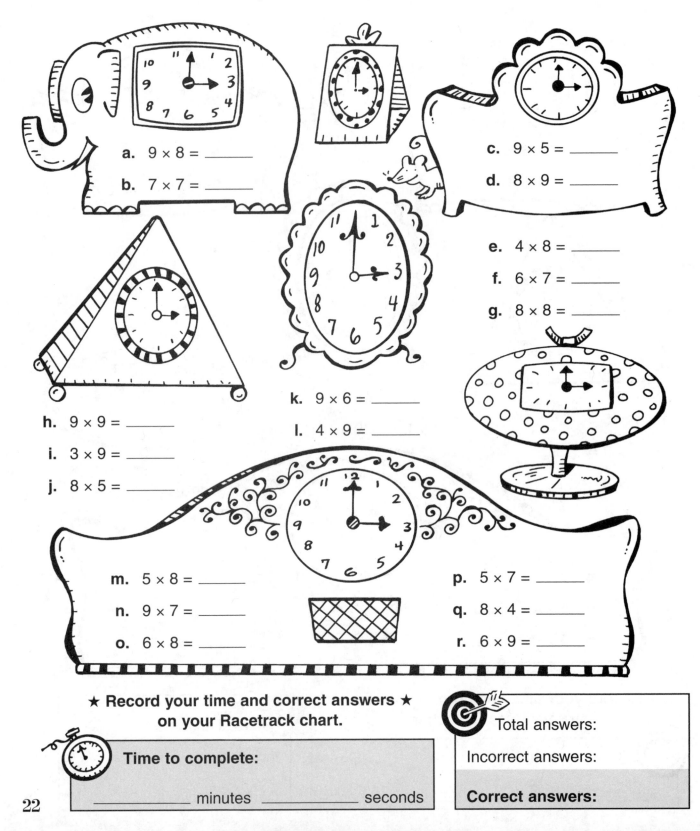

a. $9 \times 8 =$ _____

b. $7 \times 7 =$ _____

c. $9 \times 5 =$ _____

d. $8 \times 9 =$ _____

e. $4 \times 8 =$ _____

f. $6 \times 7 =$ _____

g. $8 \times 8 =$ _____

h. $9 \times 9 =$ _____

i. $3 \times 9 =$ _____

j. $8 \times 5 =$ _____

k. $9 \times 6 =$ _____

l. $4 \times 9 =$ _____

m. $5 \times 8 =$ _____

n. $9 \times 7 =$ _____

o. $6 \times 8 =$ _____

p. $5 \times 7 =$ _____

q. $8 \times 4 =$ _____

r. $6 \times 9 =$ _____

★ **Record your time and correct answers** ★
on your Racetrack chart.

Time to complete:

_____ minutes _____ seconds

Total answers:

Incorrect answers:

Correct answers:

Fast Facts: Multiplication & Division Scholastic Teaching Resources

Name _____   Date _____

Time for Times!

What time is it? Time to time doing times! Solve the problems. *Try to get those facts fast!*

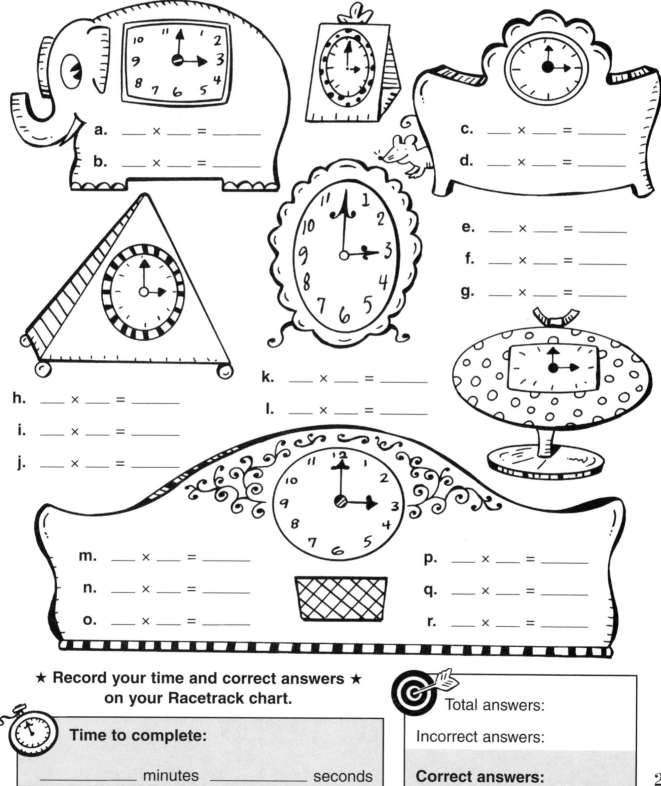

a. ___ × ___ = ___

b. ___ × ___ = ___

c. ___ × ___ = ___

d. ___ × ___ = ___

e. ___ × ___ = ___

f. ___ × ___ = ___

g. ___ × ___ = ___

h. ___ × ___ = ___

i. ___ × ___ = ___

j. ___ × ___ = ___

k. ___ × ___ = ___

l. ___ × ___ = ___

m. ___ × ___ = ___

n. ___ × ___ = ___

o. ___ × ___ = ___

p. ___ × ___ = ___

q. ___ × ___ = ___

r. ___ × ___ = ___

★ **Record your time and correct answers ★
on your Racetrack chart.**

Time to complete:

_____ minutes _____ seconds

Total answers:

Incorrect answers:

Correct answers:

Fast Facts: Multiplication & Division   Scholastic Teaching Resources

Name _____ Date _____

Divisio's Magic Show

What mathematical tricks can you perform as assistant to Divisio the Magician?
Solve the problems as they appear from Divisio's magic hat. *Try to get those facts fast!*

a. $2 \div 2 =$ _____

b. $15 \div 3 =$ _____

c. $8 \div 4 =$ _____

d. $15 \div 5 =$ _____

e. $3 \div 1 =$ _____

f. $14 \div 2 =$ _____

g. $18 \div 3 =$ _____

h. $16 \div 4 =$ _____

i. $25 \div 5 =$ _____

j. $10 \div 2 =$ _____

k. $6 \div 3 =$ _____

l. $8 \div 1 =$ _____

m. $12 \div 2 =$ _____

n. $10 \div 5 =$ _____

o. $4 \div 2 =$ _____

p. $9 \div 3 =$ _____

q. $12 \div 4 =$ _____

r. $20 \div 5 =$ _____

★ **Record your time and correct answers** ★
on your Racetrack chart.

Time to complete:

_____ minutes _____ seconds

Total answers:

Incorrect answers:

Correct answers:

Fast Facts: Multiplication & Division Scholastic Teaching Resources

Divisio's Magic Show

What mathematical tricks can you perform as assistant to Divisio the Magician?
Solve the problems as they appear from Divisio's magic hat. *Try to get those facts fast!*

a. $18 \div 6 =$ _____

b. $40 \div 8 =$ _____

c. $36 \div 4 =$ _____

d. $16 \div 2 =$ _____

e. $21 \div 7 =$ _____

f. $24 \div 8 =$ _____

g. $35 \div 5 =$ _____

h. $24 \div 3 =$ _____

i. $32 \div 8 =$ _____

j. $18 \div 9 =$ _____

k. $35 \div 7 =$ _____

l. $27 \div 3 =$ _____

m. $24 \div 6 =$ _____

n. $45 \div 9 =$ _____

o. $18 \div 2 =$ _____

p. $24 \div 4 =$ _____

q. $30 \div 5 =$ _____

r. $27 \div 9 =$ _____

★ **Record your time and correct answers** ★
on your Racetrack chart.

Time to complete:

_____ minutes _____ seconds

Total answers:

Incorrect answers:

Correct answers:

Fast Facts: Multiplication & Division Scholastic Teaching Resources

Name _____ Date _____

Divisio's Magic Show

What mathematical tricks can you perform as assistant to Divisio the Magician?
Solve the problems as they appear from Divisio's magic hat. *Try to get those facts fast!*

a. 35 ÷ 7 = _____

b. 81 ÷ 9 = _____

c. 36 ÷ 4 = _____

d. 63 ÷ 7 = _____

e. 40 ÷ 8 = _____

f. 35 ÷ 5 = _____

g. 56 ÷ 7 = _____

h. 42 ÷ 6 = _____

i. 72 ÷ 9 = _____

j. 32 ÷ 4 = _____

k. 45 ÷ 9 = _____

l. 30 ÷ 6 = _____

m. 48 ÷ 6 = _____

n. 40 ÷ 5 = _____

o. 54 ÷ 9 = _____

p. 42 ÷ 7 = _____

q. 48 ÷ 8 = _____

r. 64 ÷ 8 = _____

★ **Record your time and correct answers** ★
on your Racetrack chart.

Time to complete:

_____ minutes _____ seconds

Total answers: _____

Incorrect answers: _____

Correct answers: _____

26

Divisio's Magic Show

What mathematical tricks can you perform as assistant to Divisio the Magician?
Solve the problems as they appear from Divisio's magic hat. *Try to get those facts fast!*

a. ___ ÷ ___ = _____
b. ___ ÷ ___ = _____

c. ___ ÷ ___ = _____
d. ___ ÷ ___ = _____

e. ___ ÷ ___ = _____
f. ___ ÷ ___ = _____

g. ___ ÷ ___ = _____
h. ___ ÷ ___ = _____

i. ___ ÷ ___ = _____
j. ___ ÷ ___ = _____

k. ___ ÷ ___ = _____
l. ___ ÷ ___ = _____

m. ___ ÷ ___ = _____
n. ___ ÷ ___ = _____

o. ___ ÷ ___ = _____
p. ___ ÷ ___ = _____

q. ___ ÷ ___ = _____
r. ___ ÷ ___ = _____

★ **Record your time and correct answers** ★
on your Racetrack chart.

Time to complete:

_____ minutes _____ seconds

Total answers:

Incorrect answers:

Correct answers:

Split Snack

How do you split such a delicious treat? Divide, then dig in! *Try to get those facts fast!*

a. 14 ÷ 2 = _____

b. 25 ÷ 5 = _____

c. 2 ÷ 1 = _____

d. 4 ÷ 4 = _____

e. 9 ÷ 3 = _____

f. 20 ÷ 4 = _____

g. 6 ÷ 2 = _____

h. 10 ÷ 5 = _____

i. 1 ÷ 1 = _____

j. 8 ÷ 1 = _____

k. 8 ÷ 4 = _____

l. 20 ÷ 5 = _____

m. 12 ÷ 4 = _____

n. 5 ÷ 1 = _____

o. 12 ÷ 3 = _____

p. 16 ÷ 4 = _____

q. 8 ÷ 2 = _____

r. 21 ÷ 3 = _____

★ **Record your time and correct answers ★
on your Racetrack chart.**

Time to complete:

_____ minutes _____ seconds

Total answers:

Incorrect answers:

Correct answers:

Fast Facts: Multiplication & Division Scholastic Teaching Resources

Split Snack

How do you split such a delicious treat? Divide, then dig in! *Try to get those facts fast!*

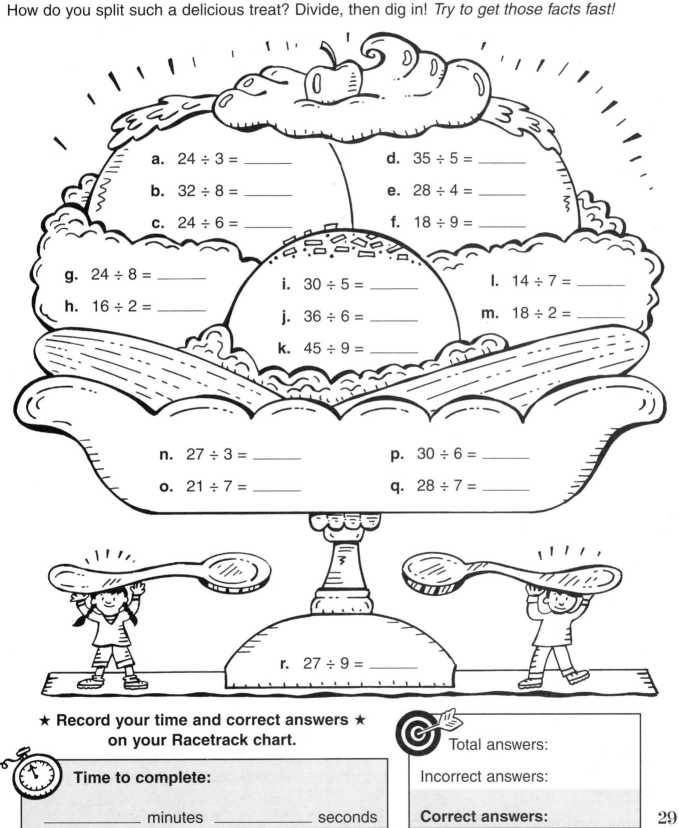

a. 24 ÷ 3 = _____

b. 32 ÷ 8 = _____

c. 24 ÷ 6 = _____

d. 35 ÷ 5 = _____

e. 28 ÷ 4 = _____

f. 18 ÷ 9 = _____

g. 24 ÷ 8 = _____

h. 16 ÷ 2 = _____

i. 30 ÷ 5 = _____

j. 36 ÷ 6 = _____

k. 45 ÷ 9 = _____

l. 14 ÷ 7 = _____

m. 18 ÷ 2 = _____

n. 27 ÷ 3 = _____

o. 21 ÷ 7 = _____

p. 30 ÷ 6 = _____

q. 28 ÷ 7 = _____

r. 27 ÷ 9 = _____

★ **Record your time and correct answers** ★
on your Racetrack chart.

Time to complete:

_____ minutes _____ seconds

Total answers: _____

Incorrect answers: _____

Correct answers: _____

Fast Facts: Multiplication & Division Scholastic Teaching Resources

Split Snack

How do you split such a delicious treat? Divide, then dig in! *Try to get those facts fast!*

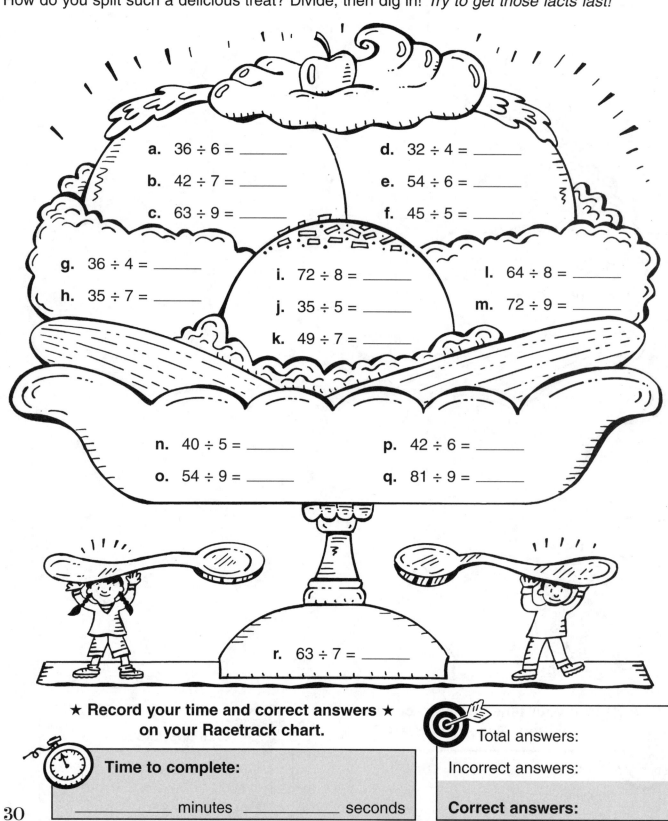

a. 36 ÷ 6 = _____

b. 42 ÷ 7 = _____

c. 63 ÷ 9 = _____

d. 32 ÷ 4 = _____

e. 54 ÷ 6 = _____

f. 45 ÷ 5 = _____

g. 36 ÷ 4 = _____

h. 35 ÷ 7 = _____

i. 72 ÷ 8 = _____

j. 35 ÷ 5 = _____

k. 49 ÷ 7 = _____

l. 64 ÷ 8 = _____

m. 72 ÷ 9 = _____

n. 40 ÷ 5 = _____

o. 54 ÷ 9 = _____

p. 42 ÷ 6 = _____

q. 81 ÷ 9 = _____

r. 63 ÷ 7 = _____

★ **Record your time and correct answers** ★
on your Racetrack chart.

Time to complete:

_____ minutes _____ seconds

Total answers:

Incorrect answers:

Correct answers:

Fast Facts: Multiplication & Division Scholastic Teaching Resources

Name _____ Date _____

How do you split such a delicious treat? Divide, then dig in! *Try to get those facts fast!*

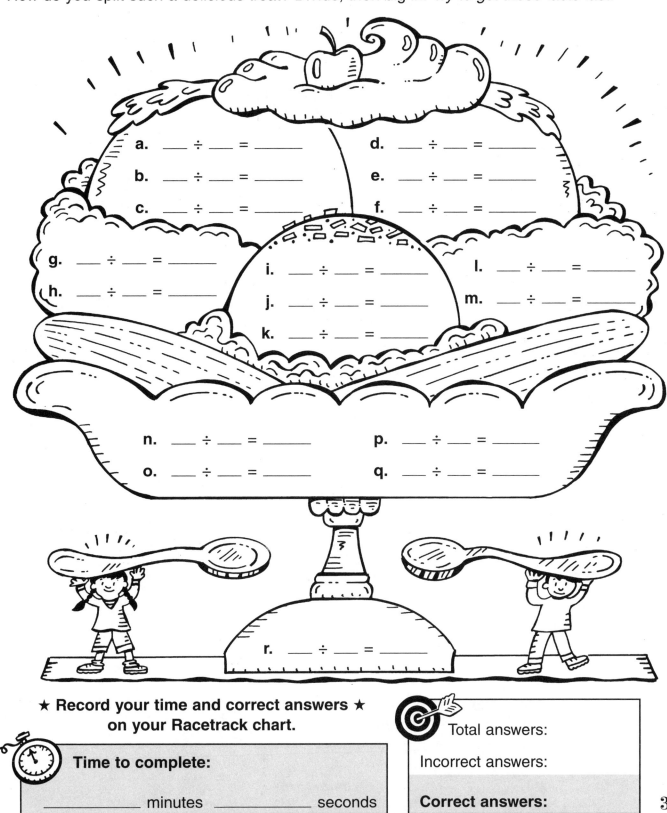

a. ____ ÷ ____ = ____

b. ____ ÷ ____ = ____

c. ____ ÷ ____ = ____

d. ____ ÷ ____ = ____

e. ____ ÷ ____ = ____

f. ____ ÷ ____ = ____

g. ____ ÷ ____ = ____

h. ____ ÷ ____ = ____

i. ____ ÷ ____ = ____

j. ____ ÷ ____ = ____

k. ____ ÷ ____ = ____

l. ____ ÷ ____ = ____

m. ____ ÷ ____ = ____

n. ____ ÷ ____ = ____

o. ____ ÷ ____ = ____

p. ____ ÷ ____ = ____

q. ____ ÷ ____ = ____

r. ____ ÷ ____ = ____

★ **Record your time and correct answers ★
on your Racetrack chart.**

Time to complete:

_____ minutes _____ seconds

Total answers: _____

Incorrect answers: _____

Correct answers: _____

Name _____ Date _____

Divide and Conquer

Can you conquer the mountain by solving all the problems?
Try to get those facts fast!

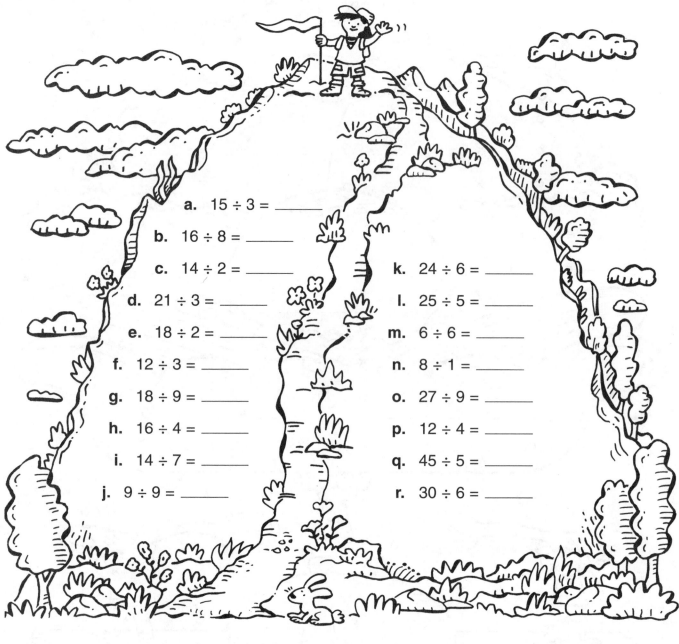

a. $15 \div 3 =$ _____

b. $16 \div 8 =$ _____

c. $14 \div 2 =$ _____

d. $21 \div 3 =$ _____

e. $18 \div 2 =$ _____

f. $12 \div 3 =$ _____

g. $18 \div 9 =$ _____

h. $16 \div 4 =$ _____

i. $14 \div 7 =$ _____

j. $9 \div 9 =$ _____

k. $24 \div 6 =$ _____

l. $25 \div 5 =$ _____

m. $6 \div 6 =$ _____

n. $8 \div 1 =$ _____

o. $27 \div 9 =$ _____

p. $12 \div 4 =$ _____

q. $45 \div 5 =$ _____

r. $30 \div 6 =$ _____

★ **Record your time and correct answers** ★
on your Racetrack chart.

Time to complete:

_____ minutes _____ seconds

Total answers: _____

Incorrect answers: _____

Correct answers: _____

32

Divide and Conquer

Can you conquer the mountain by solving all the problems?
Try to get those facts fast!

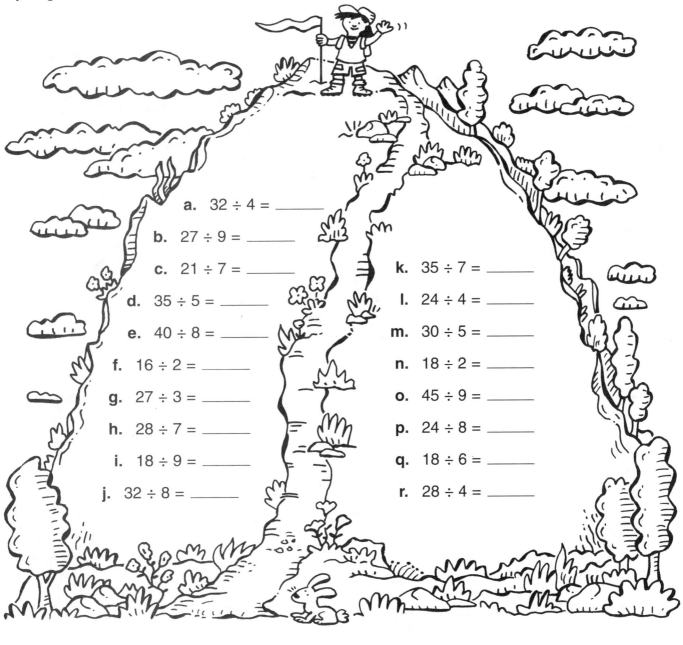

a. 32 ÷ 4 = _____

b. 27 ÷ 9 = _____

c. 21 ÷ 7 = _____

d. 35 ÷ 5 = _____

e. 40 ÷ 8 = _____

f. 16 ÷ 2 = _____

g. 27 ÷ 3 = _____

h. 28 ÷ 7 = _____

i. 18 ÷ 9 = _____

j. 32 ÷ 8 = _____

k. 35 ÷ 7 = _____

l. 24 ÷ 4 = _____

m. 30 ÷ 5 = _____

n. 18 ÷ 2 = _____

o. 45 ÷ 9 = _____

p. 24 ÷ 8 = _____

q. 18 ÷ 6 = _____

r. 28 ÷ 4 = _____

★ **Record your time and correct answers** ★
on your Racetrack chart.

Time to complete:

_____ minutes _____ seconds

Total answers:

Incorrect answers:

Correct answers:

Fast Facts: Multiplication & Division Scholastic Teaching Resources

Name _____   Date _____

Divide and Conquer

Can you conquer the mountain by solving all the problems?
Try to get those facts fast!

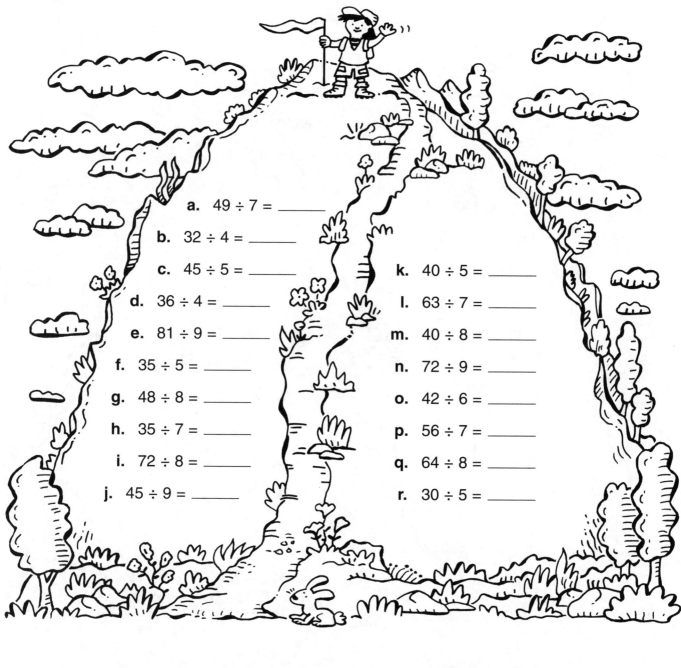

a. $49 \div 7 =$ _____

b. $32 \div 4 =$ _____

c. $45 \div 5 =$ _____

d. $36 \div 4 =$ _____

e. $81 \div 9 =$ _____

f. $35 \div 5 =$ _____

g. $48 \div 8 =$ _____

h. $35 \div 7 =$ _____

i. $72 \div 8 =$ _____

j. $45 \div 9 =$ _____

k. $40 \div 5 =$ _____

l. $63 \div 7 =$ _____

m. $40 \div 8 =$ _____

n. $72 \div 9 =$ _____

o. $42 \div 6 =$ _____

p. $56 \div 7 =$ _____

q. $64 \div 8 =$ _____

r. $30 \div 5 =$ _____

★ **Record your time and correct answers** ★
on your Racetrack chart.

Time to complete:

_____ minutes _____ seconds

Total answers: _____

Incorrect answers: _____

Correct answers:

34

Divide and Conquer

Can you conquer the mountain by solving all the problems?
Try to get those facts fast!

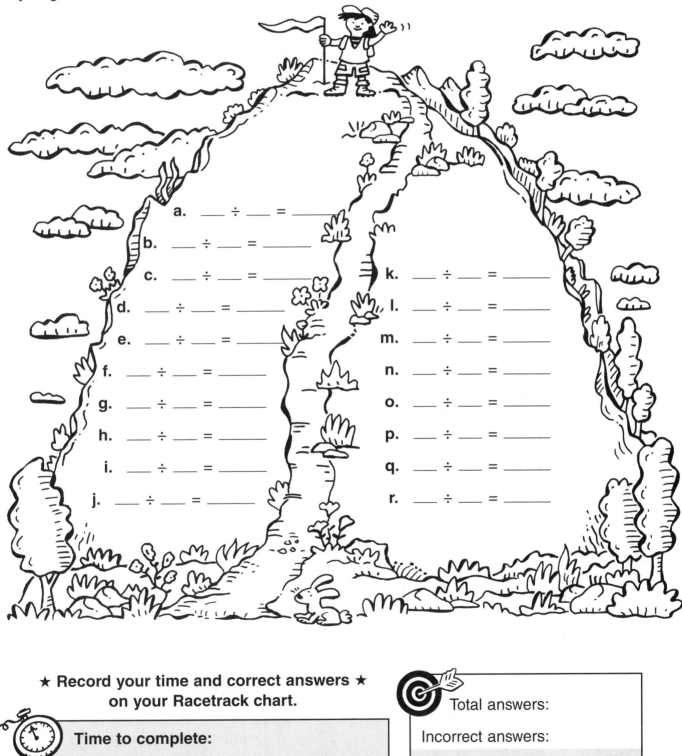

a. ___ ÷ ___ = ___

b. ___ ÷ ___ = ___

c. ___ ÷ ___ = ___   k. ___ ÷ ___ = ___

d. ___ ÷ ___ = ___   l. ___ ÷ ___ = ___

e. ___ ÷ ___ = ___   m. ___ ÷ ___ = ___

f. ___ ÷ ___ = ___   n. ___ ÷ ___ = ___

g. ___ ÷ ___ = ___   o. ___ ÷ ___ = ___

h. ___ ÷ ___ = ___   p. ___ ÷ ___ = ___

i. ___ ÷ ___ = ___   q. ___ ÷ ___ = ___

j. ___ ÷ ___ = ___   r. ___ ÷ ___ = ___

★ **Record your time and correct answers** ★
on your Racetrack chart.

Time to complete:

_____ minutes _____ seconds

Total answers:

Incorrect answers:

Correct answers:

Dividing Lines

Make your way down the field by solving the problems. If you get them right, it's a touchdown for your team! *Try to get those facts fast!*

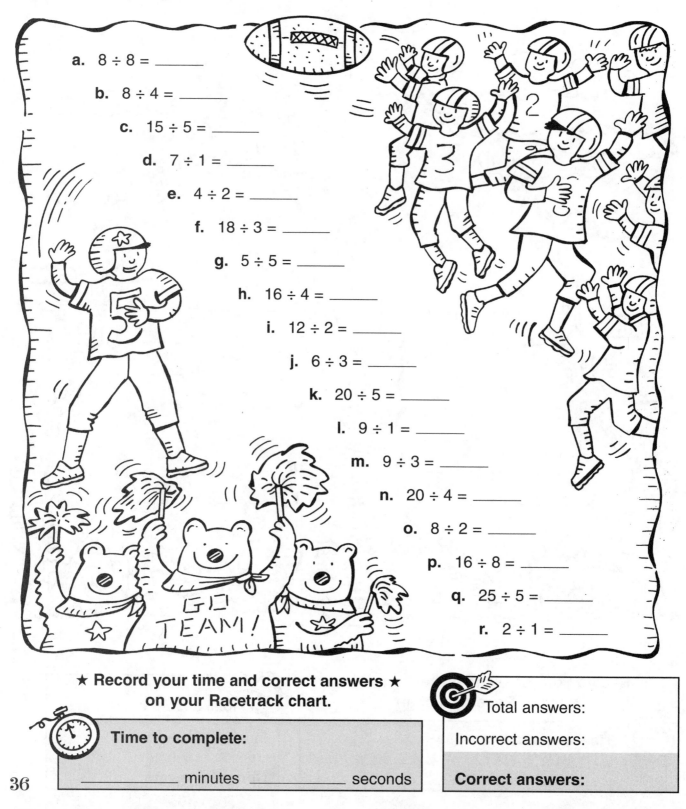

a. $8 \div 8 =$ _____

b. $8 \div 4 =$ _____

c. $15 \div 5 =$ _____

d. $7 \div 1 =$ _____

e. $4 \div 2 =$ _____

f. $18 \div 3 =$ _____

g. $5 \div 5 =$ _____

h. $16 \div 4 =$ _____

i. $12 \div 2 =$ _____

j. $6 \div 3 =$ _____

k. $20 \div 5 =$ _____

l. $9 \div 1 =$ _____

m. $9 \div 3 =$ _____

n. $20 \div 4 =$ _____

o. $8 \div 2 =$ _____

p. $16 \div 8 =$ _____

q. $25 \div 5 =$ _____

r. $2 \div 1 =$ _____

GO TEAM!

★ **Record your time and correct answers** ★
on your Racetrack chart.

Time to complete:

_____ minutes _____ seconds

Total answers: _____

Incorrect answers: _____

Correct answers: _____

Fast Facts: Multiplication & Division Scholastic Teaching Resources

Name _____   Date _____

Dividing Lines

Make your way down the field by solving the problems. If you get them right, it's a touchdown for your team! *Try to get those facts fast!*

a. $32 \div 4 =$ _____

b. $18 \div 9 =$ _____

c. $30 \div 5 =$ _____

d. $18 \div 2 =$ _____

e. $27 \div 9 =$ _____

f. $40 \div 8 =$ _____

g. $24 \div 4 =$ _____

h. $36 \div 9 =$ _____

i. $16 \div 2 =$ _____

j. $36 \div 4 =$ _____

k. $28 \div 4 =$ _____

l. $35 \div 5 =$ _____

m. $21 \div 7 =$ _____

n. $27 \div 3 =$ _____

o. $32 \div 8 =$ _____

p. $30 \div 6 =$ _____

q. $45 \div 9 =$ _____

r. $24 \div 6 =$ _____

★ **Record your time and correct answers** ★
on your Racetrack chart.

Time to complete:

_____ minutes _____ seconds

Total answers:

Incorrect answers:

Correct answers:

Fast Facts: Multiplication & Division Scholastic Teaching Resources

Dividing Lines

Make your way down the field by solving the problems. If you get them right, it's a touchdown for your team! *Try to get those facts fast!*

a. $81 \div 9 =$ _____

b. $35 \div 5 =$ _____

c. $48 \div 8 =$ _____

d. $36 \div 4 =$ _____

e. $35 \div 5 =$ _____

f. $49 \div 7 =$ _____

g. $36 \div 6 =$ _____

h. $72 \div 9 =$ _____

i. $54 \div 9 =$ _____

j. $30 \div 6 =$ _____

k. $40 \div 5 =$ _____

l. $63 \div 7 =$ _____

m. $45 \div 5 =$ _____

n. $54 \div 6 =$ _____

o. $32 \div 4 =$ _____

p. $42 \div 7 =$ _____

q. $40 \div 8 =$ _____

r. $63 \div 9 =$ _____

★ **Record your time and correct answers** ★
on your Racetrack chart.

Total answers:

Incorrect answers:

Time to complete:

Correct answers:

_____ minutes _____ seconds

Fast Facts: Multiplication & Division Scholastic Teaching Resources

Dividing Lines

Make your way down the field by solving the problems. If you get them right, it's a touchdown for your team! *Try to get those facts fast!*

a. ___ ÷ ___ = _____

b. ___ ÷ ___ = _____

c. ___ ÷ ___ = _____

d. ___ ÷ ___ = _____

e. ___ ÷ ___ = _____

f. ___ ÷ ___ = _____

g. ___ ÷ ___ = _____

h. ___ ÷ ___ = _____

i. ___ ÷ ___ = _____

j. ___ ÷ ___ = _____

k. ___ ÷ ___ = _____

l. ___ ÷ ___ = _____

m. ___ ÷ ___ = _____

n. ___ ÷ ___ = _____

o. ___ ÷ ___ = _____

p. ___ ÷ ___ = _____

q. ___ ÷ ___ = _____

r. ___ ÷ ___ = _____

★ **Record your time and correct answers** ★
on your Racetrack chart.

Time to complete:

_____ minutes _____ seconds

Total answers: _____

Incorrect answers: _____

Correct answers: _____

Fast Facts: Multiplication & Division Scholastic Teaching Resources

Name _____ Date _____

The Division Times

Read all about it! Do the division and the multiplication problems that are hot off the press. *Try to get those facts fast!*

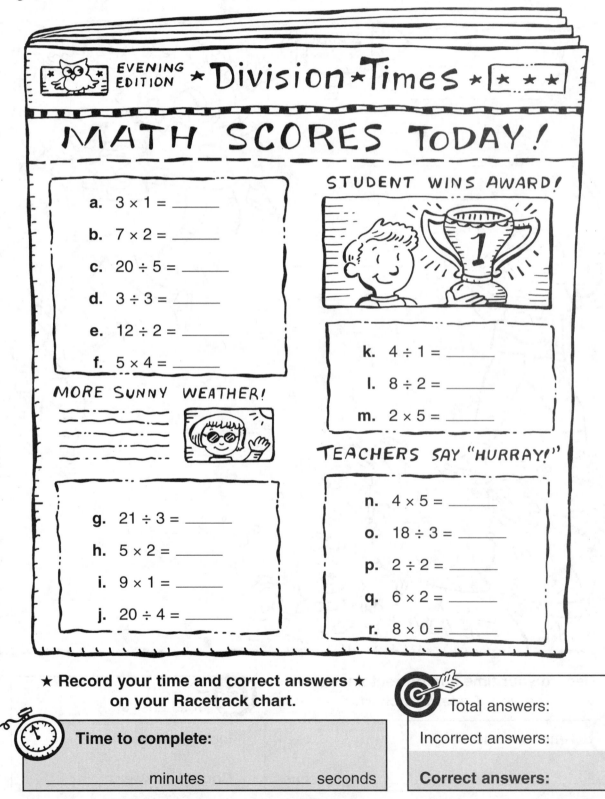

EVENING EDITION ★ Division ★ Times ★

MATH SCORES TODAY!

a. $3 \times 1 =$ _____

b. $7 \times 2 =$ _____

c. $20 \div 5 =$ _____

d. $3 \div 3 =$ _____

e. $12 \div 2 =$ _____

f. $5 \times 4 =$ _____

MORE SUNNY WEATHER!

g. $21 \div 3 =$ _____

h. $5 \times 2 =$ _____

i. $9 \times 1 =$ _____

j. $20 \div 4 =$ _____

STUDENT WINS AWARD!

k. $4 \div 1 =$ _____

l. $8 \div 2 =$ _____

m. $2 \times 5 =$ _____

TEACHERS SAY "HURRAY!"

n. $4 \times 5 =$ _____

o. $18 \div 3 =$ _____

p. $2 \div 2 =$ _____

q. $6 \times 2 =$ _____

r. $8 \times 0 =$ _____

★ **Record your time and correct answers** ★
on your Racetrack chart.

Time to complete:

_____ minutes _____ seconds

Total answers: _____

Incorrect answers: _____

Correct answers: _____

40

Fast Facts: Multiplication & Division Scholastic Teaching Resources

Name _____   Date _____

The Division Times

Read all about it! Do the division and the multiplication problems that are hot off the press.
Try to get those facts fast!

EVENING EDITION ★ Division ★ Times ★ ★ ★ ★

MATH SCORES TODAY!

a. $2 \times 9 =$ _____

b. $36 \div 6 =$ _____

c. $18 \div 9 =$ _____

d. $9 \times 2 =$ _____

e. $24 \div 4 =$ _____

f. $18 \div 6 =$ _____

MORE SUNNY WEATHER!

g. $3 \times 8 =$ _____

h. $7 \times 3 =$ _____

i. $40 \div 8 =$ _____

j. $27 \div 9 =$ _____

STUDENT WINS AWARD!

k. $5 \times 6 =$ _____

l. $27 \div 3 =$ _____

m. $12 \div 6 =$ _____

TEACHERS SAY "HURRAY!"

n. $7 \times 5 =$ _____

o. $32 \div 8 =$ _____

p. $7 \times 6 =$ _____

q. $5 \times 5 =$ _____

r. $18 \div 2 =$ _____

★ **Record your time and correct answers** ★
on your Racetrack chart.

Time to complete:

_____ minutes _____ seconds

Total answers:

Incorrect answers:

Correct answers:

Name _____   Date _____

The Division Times

Read all about it! Do the division and the multiplication problems that are hot off the press.
Try to get those facts fast!

EVENING EDITION ★ Division ★ Times ★

MATH SCORES TODAY!

a. $7 \times 7 =$ _____

b. $30 \div 6 =$ _____

c. $42 \div 7 =$ _____

d. $81 \div 9 =$ _____

e. $3 \times 9 =$ _____

f. $32 \div 8 =$ _____

MORE SUNNY WEATHER!

g. $6 \times 9 =$ _____

h. $9 \times 5 =$ _____

i. $40 \div 5 =$ _____

j. $36 \div 6 =$ _____

STUDENT WINS AWARD!

k. $8 \times 9 =$ _____

l. $36 \div 4 =$ _____

m. $42 \div 6 =$ _____

TEACHERS SAY "HURRAY!"

n. $5 \times 9 =$ _____

o. $8 \times 4 =$ _____

p. $72 \div 8 =$ _____

q. $4 \times 7 =$ _____

r. $49 \div 7 =$ _____

★ **Record your time and correct answers** ★
on your Racetrack chart.

Time to complete:

_____ minutes _____ seconds

Total answers:

Incorrect answers:

Correct answers:

Fast Facts: Multiplication & Division Scholastic Teaching Resources

The Division Times

Read all about it! Do the division and the multiplication problems that are hot off the press. *Try to get those facts fast!*

EVENING EDITION ★ Division ★ Times ★ ★ ★ ★

MATH SCORES TODAY!

a. ___ × ___ = _____

b. ___ ÷ ___ = _____

c. ___ × ___ = _____

d. ___ ÷ ___ = _____

e. ___ × ___ = _____

f. ___ ÷ ___ = _____

STUDENT WINS AWARD!

k. ___ × ___ = _____

l. ___ ÷ ___ = _____

m. ___ × ___ = _____

MORE SUNNY WEATHER!

g. ___ × ___ = _____

h. ___ ÷ ___ = _____

i. ___ × ___ = _____

j. ___ ÷ ___ = _____

TEACHERS SAY "HURRAY!"

n. ___ ÷ ___ = _____

o. ___ × ___ = _____

p. ___ ÷ ___ = _____

q. ___ × ___ = _____

r. ___ ÷ ___ = _____

★ **Record your time and correct answers** ★
on your Racetrack chart.

Time to complete:

_____ minutes _____ seconds

Total answers:

Incorrect answers:

Correct answers:

Fast Facts: Multiplication & Division Scholastic Teaching Resources

Name _____ Date _____

Divide the X-tra

Giving out slices of that x-cellent, x-traordinary pizza? Divide and multiply so everyone can dig in! *Try to get those facts fast!*

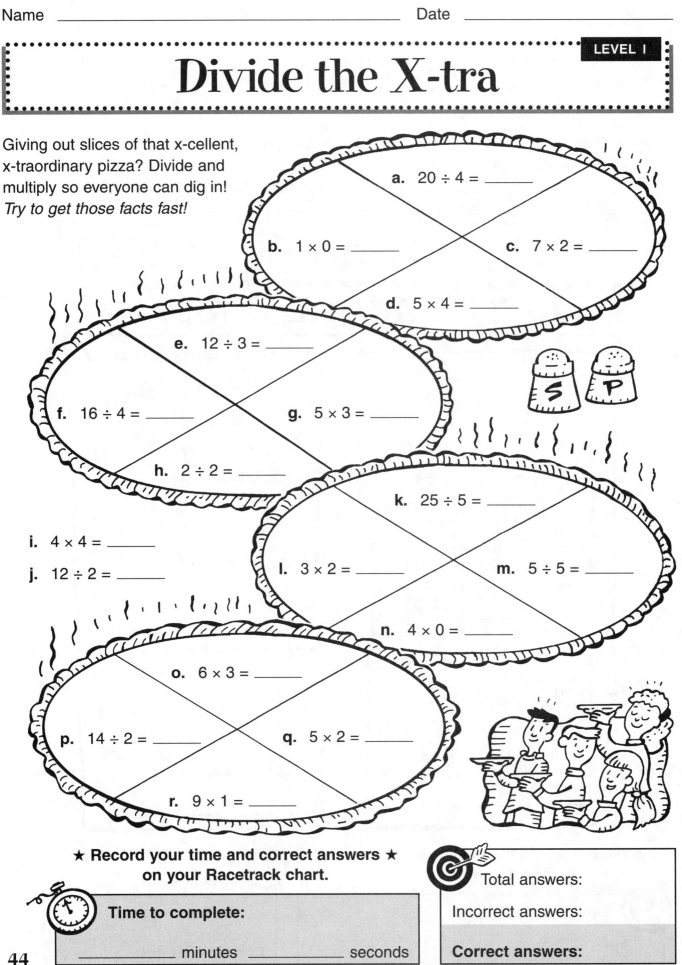

a. 20 ÷ 4 = _____

b. 1 × 0 = _____

c. 7 × 2 = _____

d. 5 × 4 = _____

e. 12 ÷ 3 = _____

f. 16 ÷ 4 = _____

g. 5 × 3 = _____

h. 2 ÷ 2 = _____

i. 4 × 4 = _____

j. 12 ÷ 2 = _____

k. 25 ÷ 5 = _____

l. 3 × 2 = _____

m. 5 ÷ 5 = _____

n. 4 × 0 = _____

o. 6 × 3 = _____

p. 14 ÷ 2 = _____

q. 5 × 2 = _____

r. 9 × 1 = _____

★ **Record your time and correct answers** ★
on your Racetrack chart.

Total answers: _____

Incorrect answers: _____

Time to complete:

_____ minutes _____ seconds

Correct answers: _____

44

Fast Facts: Multiplication & Division Scholastic Teaching Resources

Name _____   Date _____

Divide the X-tra

Giving out slices of that x-cellent, x-traordinary pizza? Divide and multiply so everyone can dig in! *Try to get those facts fast!*

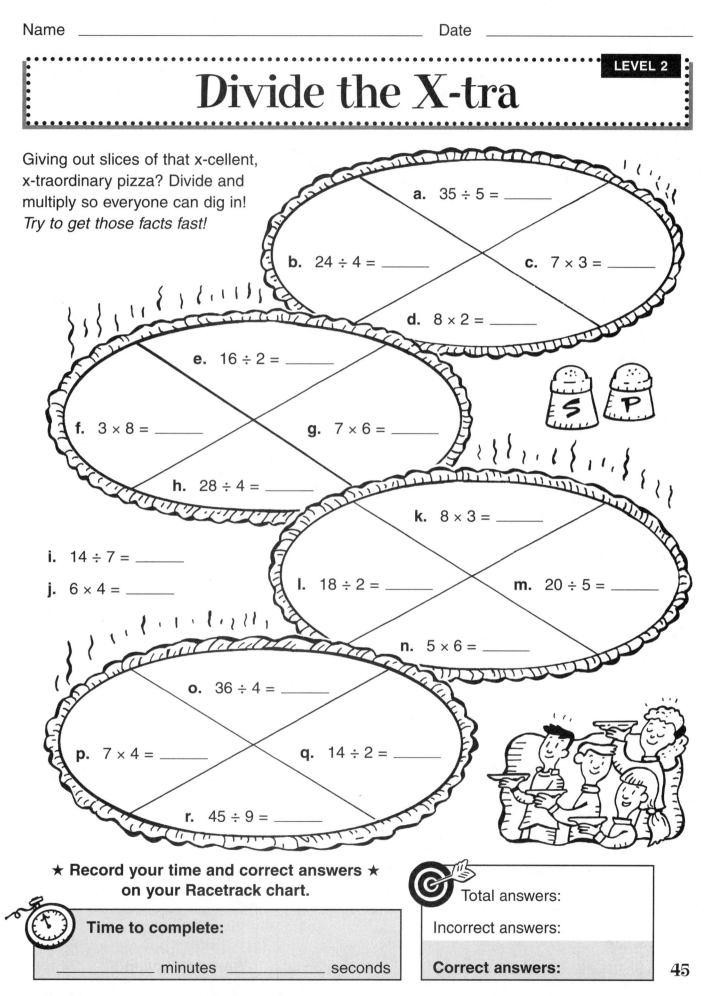

a. $35 \div 5 =$ _____

b. $24 \div 4 =$ _____

c. $7 \times 3 =$ _____

d. $8 \times 2 =$ _____

e. $16 \div 2 =$ _____

f. $3 \times 8 =$ _____

g. $7 \times 6 =$ _____

h. $28 \div 4 =$ _____

i. $14 \div 7 =$ _____

j. $6 \times 4 =$ _____

k. $8 \times 3 =$ _____

l. $18 \div 2 =$ _____

m. $20 \div 5 =$ _____

n. $5 \times 6 =$ _____

o. $36 \div 4 =$ _____

p. $7 \times 4 =$ _____

q. $14 \div 2 =$ _____

r. $45 \div 9 =$ _____

★ **Record your time and correct answers** ★
on your Racetrack chart.

Time to complete:

_____ minutes _____ seconds

Total answers:

Incorrect answers:

Correct answers:

LEVEL 3

Divide the X-tra

Giving out slices of that x-cellent, x-traordinary pizza? Divide and multiply so everyone can dig in! *Try to get those facts fast!*

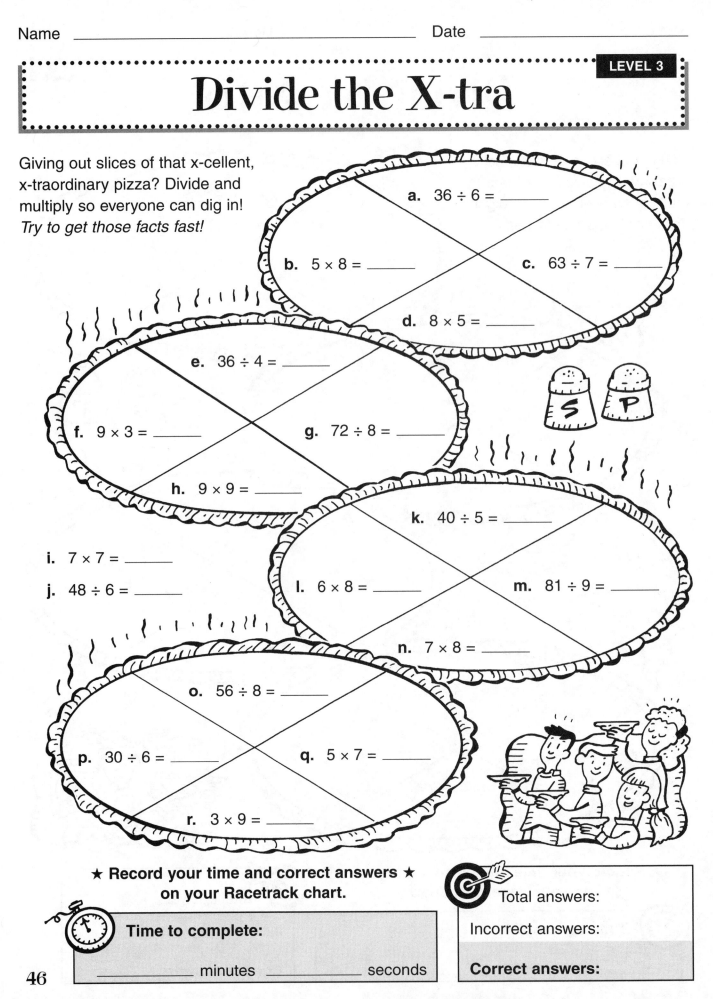

a. $36 \div 6 =$ _____

b. $5 \times 8 =$ _____

c. $63 \div 7 =$ _____

d. $8 \times 5 =$ _____

e. $36 \div 4 =$ _____

f. $9 \times 3 =$ _____

g. $72 \div 8 =$ _____

h. $9 \times 9 =$ _____

i. $7 \times 7 =$ _____

j. $48 \div 6 =$ _____

k. $40 \div 5 =$ _____

l. $6 \times 8 =$ _____

m. $81 \div 9 =$ _____

n. $7 \times 8 =$ _____

o. $56 \div 8 =$ _____

p. $30 \div 6 =$ _____

q. $5 \times 7 =$ _____

r. $3 \times 9 =$ _____

★ **Record your time and correct answers** ★
on your Racetrack chart.

Time to complete:

_____ minutes _____ seconds

Total answers:

Incorrect answers:

Correct answers:

46

Fast Facts: Multiplication & Division Scholastic Teaching Resources

Divide the X-tra

Giving out slices of that x-cellent, x-traordinary pizza? Divide and multiply so everyone can dig in! *Try to get those facts fast!*

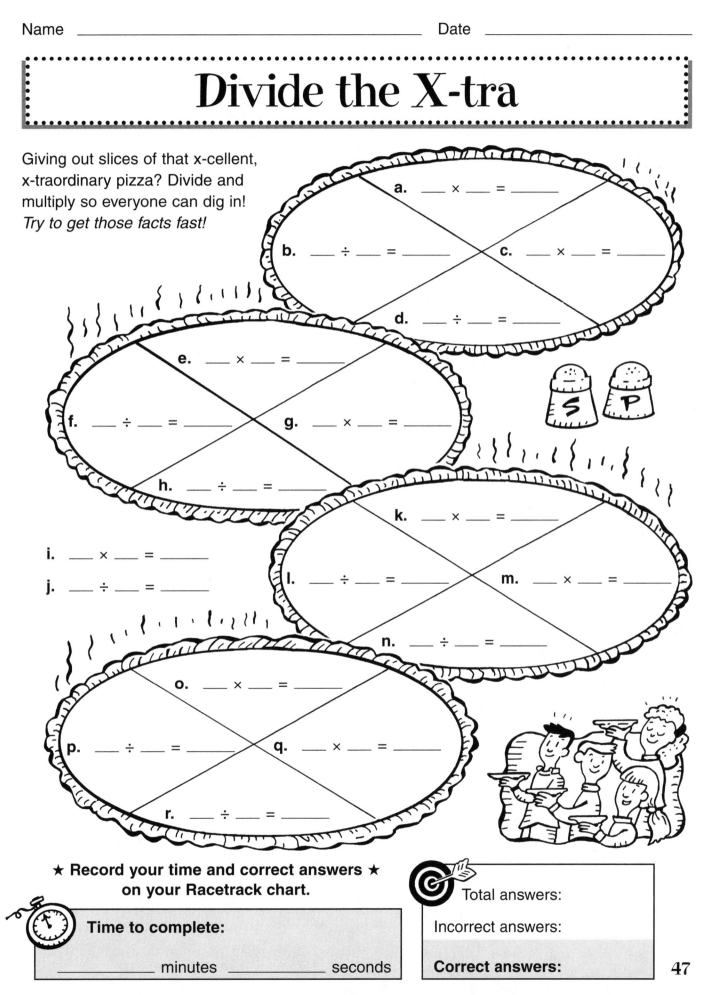

a. ___ × ___ = _____

b. ___ ÷ ___ = _____   **c.** ___ × ___ = _____

d. ___ ÷ ___ = _____

e. ___ × ___ = _____

f. ___ ÷ ___ = _____   **g.** ___ × ___ = _____

h. ___ ÷ ___ = _____

i. ___ × ___ = _____

j. ___ ÷ ___ = _____

k. ___ × ___ = _____

l. ___ ÷ ___ = _____   **m.** ___ × ___ = _____

n. ___ ÷ ___ = _____

o. ___ × ___ = _____

p. ___ ÷ ___ = _____   **q.** ___ × ___ = _____

r. ___ ÷ ___ = _____

★ **Record your time and correct answers** ★
on your Racetrack chart.

Time to complete:

_____ minutes _____ seconds

Total answers:

Incorrect answers:

Correct answers:

Answer Key

Multiplication

Page 8	Page 12	Page 16	Page 20
a. 6	a. 15	a. 3	a. 18
b. 0	b. 9	b. 10	b. 8
c. 5	c. 12	c. 0	c. 14
d. 8	d. 15	d. 12	d. 12
e. 15	e. 6	e. 7	e. 0
f. 12	f. 14	f. 0	f. 10
g. 10	g. 0	g. 15	g. 12
h. 16	h. 20	h. 8	h. 12
i. 6	i. 7	i. 6	i. 6
j. 0	j. 12	j. 0	j. 15
k. 9	k. 10	k. 12	k. 0
l. 20	l. 4	l. 3	l. 20
m. 12	m. 0	m. 12	m. 12
n. 12	n. 9	n. 4	n. 16
o. 15	o. 8	o. 20	o. 9
p. 14	p. 8	p. 0	p. 0
q. 0	q. 18	q. 21	q. 4
r. 9	r. 0	r. 9	r. 8

Page 9	Page 13	Page 17	Page 21
a. 24	a. 18	a. 24	a. 24
b. 18	b. 30	b. 14	b. 25
c. 24	c. 16	c. 27	c. 24
d. 25	d. 42	d. 24	d. 36
e. 21	e. 25	e. 30	e. 16
f. 45	f. 24	f. 28	f. 35
g. 32	g. 28	g. 16	g. 21
h. 36	h. 24	h. 35	h. 30
i. 18	i. 30	i. 36	i. 16
j. 35	j. 21	j. 18	j. 24
k. 16	k. 24	k. 32	k. 30
l. 30	l. 35	l. 45	l. 18
m. 24	m. 18	m. 18	m. 28
n. 16	n. 16	n. 32	n. 24
o. 36	o. 21	o. 21	o. 27
p. 35	p. 28	p. 40	p. 28
q. 30	q. 36	q. 21	q. 48
r. 36	r. 18	r. 36	r. 18

Page 10	Page 14	Page 18	Page 22
a. 36	a. 45	a. 54	a. 72
b. 36	b. 48	b. 45	b. 49
c. 63	c. 63	c. 36	c. 45
d. 42	d. 35	d. 32	d. 72
e. 54	e. 54	e. 36	e. 32
f. 32	f. 36	f. 27	f. 42
g. 45	g. 49	g. 56	g. 64
h. 42	h. 40	h. 81	h. 81
i. 72	i. 32	i. 32	i. 27
j. 40	j. 81	j. 30	j. 40
k. 81	k. 56	k. 64	k. 54
l. 49	l. 27	l. 48	l. 36
m. 30	m. 40	m. 63	m. 40
n. 56	n. 42	n. 28	n. 63
o. 54	o. 56	o. 72	o. 48
p. 24	p. 48	p. 42	p. 35
q. 64	q. 72	q. 40	q. 32
r. 30	r. 36	r. 56	r. 54

Division

Page 24	Page 28	Page 32	Page 36
a. 1	a. 7	a. 5	a. 1
b. 5	b. 5	b. 2	b. 2
c. 2	c. 2	c. 7	c. 3
d. 3	d. 1	d. 7	d. 7
e. 3	e. 3	e. 9	e. 2
f. 7	f. 5	f. 4	f. 6
g. 6	g. 3	g. 2	g. 1
h. 4	h. 2	h. 4	h. 4
i. 5	i. 1	i. 2	i. 6
j. 5	j. 8	j. 1	j. 2
k. 2	k. 2	k. 4	k. 4
l. 8	l. 4	l. 5	l. 9
m. 6	m. 3	m. 1	m. 3
n. 2	n. 5	n. 8	n. 5
o. 2	o. 4	o. 4	o. 3
p. 3	p. 4	p. 4	p. 2
q. 3	q. 4	q. 9	q. 5
r. 4	r. 7	r. 5	r. 2

Page 25	Page 29	Page 33	Page 37
a. 3	a. 8	a. 8	a. 8
b. 5	b. 4	b. 3	b. 2
c. 9	c. 4	c. 3	c. 6
d. 8	d. 7	d. 7	d. 9
e. 3	e. 7	e. 5	e. 3
f. 3	f. 2	f. 8	f. 5
g. 7	g. 3	g. 9	g. 6
h. 8	h. 8	h. 4	h. 4
i. 4	i. 6	i. 2	i. 8
j. 2	j. 6	j. 4	j. 9
k. 5	k. 5	k. 5	k. 7
l. 9	l. 2	l. 2	l. 7
m. 4	m. 9	m. 6	m. 3
n. 5	n. 9	n. 9	n. 9
o. 9	o. 3	o. 5	o. 4
p. 6	p. 5	p. 3	p. 5
q. 6	q. 4	q. 3	q. 5
r. 3	r. 3	r. 7	r. 4

Page 26	Page 30	Page 34	Page 38
a. 5	a. 6	a. 7	a. 9
b. 9	b. 6	b. 8	b. 7
c. 9	c. 7	c. 9	c. 6
d. 9	d. 8	d. 9	d. 9
e. 5	e. 9	e. 9	e. 7
f. 7	f. 9	f. 7	f. 7
g. 8	g. 9	g. 6	g. 6
h. 7	h. 5	h. 5	h. 8
i. 8	i. 9	i. 9	i. 6
j. 8	j. 7	j. 5	j. 5
k. 5	k. 7	k. 8	k. 8
l. 5	l. 8	l. 9	l. 9
m. 8	m. 8	m. 5	m. 9
n. 8	n. 8	n. 8	n. 9
o. 6	o. 6	o. 7	o. 8
p. 6	p. 7	p. 8	p. 6
q. 6	q. 9	q. 8	q. 5
r. 8	r. 9	r. 6	r. 7

Multiplication/Division

Page 40	Page 44
a. 3	a. 5
b. 14	b. 0
c. 4	c. 14
d. 1	d. 20
e. 6	e. 4
f. 20	f. 4
g. 7	g. 15
h. 10	h. 1
i. 9	i. 16
j. 5	j. 6
k. 4	k. 5
l. 4	l. 6
m. 10	m. 1
n. 20	n. 0
o. 6	o. 18
p. 1	p. 7
q. 12	q. 10
r. 0	r. 9

Page 41	Page 45
a. 18	a. 7
b. 6	b. 6
c. 2	c. 21
d. 18	d. 16
e. 6	e. 8
f. 3	f. 24
g. 24	g. 42
h. 21	h. 7
i. 5	i. 2
j. 3	j. 24
k. 30	k. 24
l. 9	l. 9
m. 2	m. 4
n. 35	n. 30
o. 4	o. 9
p. 42	p. 28
q. 25	q. 7
r. 9	r. 5

Page 42	Page 46
a. 49	a. 6
b. 5	b. 40
c. 6	c. 9
d. 9	d. 40
e. 27	e. 9
f. 4	f. 27
g. 54	g. 9
h. 45	h. 81
i. 8	i. 49
j. 6	j. 8
k. 72	k. 8
l. 9	l. 48
m. 7	m. 9
n. 45	n. 56
o. 32	o. 7
p. 9	p. 5
q. 28	q. 35
r. 7	r. 27